BASEBALL

BASEBALL: FIELD & EQUIPMENT

BRYANT LLOYD

The Rourke Press, Inc.
Vero Beach, Florida 32964

PHOTO CREDITS:
All photos © Lynn M. Stone except p.22 © Rob Simpson

EDITORIAL SERVICES:
Penworthy Learning Systems

Library of Congress Cataloging-in-Publication Data

Lloyd, Bryant, 1942-
   Baseball, field & equipment / Bryant Lloyd.
     p. cm. — (Baseball)
   Includes index
   Summary: Discusses two essential elements of the game of baseball: the field on which the game is played and the equipment used in the game.
   ISBN 1-57103-185-5
   1. Baseball fields—Juvenile literature. 2. Baseball—Equipment and supplies—Juvenile literature. [1. Baseball fields. 2. Baseball—Equipment and supplies.]
I. Title II. Series: Lloyd, Bryant, 1942-   Baseball.
GV879.5.L56 1997
796.357'028—dc21   97–17455
                                         CIP
                                         AC

Printed in the USA

TABLE OF CONTENTS

BASEBALL EQUIPMENT

Regulation (reg yuh LAY shun) baseball games are played by official baseball rules. The players need certain equipment, as well as a field. A regulation game also needs the help of certain people besides players—**umpires** (UM pyrz), coaches, managers.

A basically flat baseball field is a must, also.

Big league fields differ in their outfield distances. Some of the old parks were no more than 250 feet (almost 76 meters) down the right and left field foul lines. New parks must be at least 325 feet (about 99 meters) down the lines and at least 400 feet (122 meters) in center field.

A team of Little Leaguers takes the field at the start of a game.

THE FIELD

A baseball field has an infield and an outfield in fair territory. The infield part has dirt paths between the bases and a pitcher's mound of dirt.

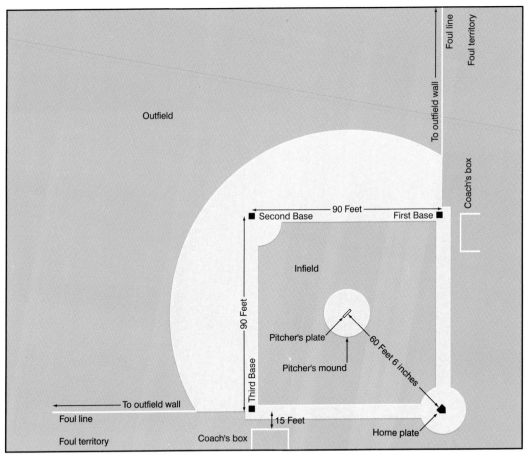

This diagram shows the basic layout of a professional baseball field.

White lines of chalk or lime mark the boundary between fair and foul territory, seen here along the first-base line.

The remainder of the infield and the outfield may be real or **artificial** (AHR tuh FISH ul) grass.

Baseball fields have white lines to separate fair territory from foul territory. Lines also mark areas on the field called batter's, catcher's, and coaches' boxes.

Some fields have **dugouts** (DUG OUTS). Dugouts are places dug into the field for players' benches.

THE BASES

Hard, rubbery home plate is one of the four bases on a baseball field. The batter stands next to home plate.

Each base is 90 feet (27 meters) away from the next. Together, the four bases form a diamond.

Except for home plate, the bases are white canvas bags. Each base is filled with soft material and anchored to the ground.

The distance between bases on a Little League field is 60 feet (18 meters).

A batter takes a pitch low for a ball at home plate, the starting point on a baseball diamond.

THE BASEBALL

A baseball is about the size of an orange, but perfectly round. It is 9 to 9 1/2 inches (23 to 24 centimeters) around. Unlike softballs, which are bigger, a baseball is almost rock-hard.

The making of a baseball begins with a small cork. The cork is wrapped with tight layers of yarn and rubber. Two cowhide sections sewn together with red thread make the cover of the ball.

Until 1974, baseballs were produced from horsehide instead of cowhide. Baseballs, like bats and gloves, are manufactured by sporting goods companies in factories.

Cowhide strips sewn together with red thread make the cover of a baseball.

BATS

Baseball bats are used by hitters to strike pitched baseballs. Bats differ in size. Little League bats are as short as 29 inches (74 centimeters). High school, college, and **professional** (pruh FESH uh nul) players generally use bats between 33 and 36 inches (84 - 91 centimeters).

Almost all baseball players who are not professional use aluminum bats.

Major Leaguers, here at a spring training workout, use wooden bats, like the shiny black one with the gloves.

Professionals, including all major leaguers, must use wood bats. Bats are made at factories, mostly of ash, but sometimes from hickory or hackberry trees.

Nonprofessionals often use **aluminum** (uh LOO muh num) bats. Aluminum tends to hit a ball harder and farther than wood.

HELMETS, GLOVES, AND SHOES

A batter wears a helmet made of hard plastic. It protects the player's head from serious injury if struck by a ball. Players also wear a helmet when they run the bases.

A baseball glove is used for fielding the baseball. It's made of padded leather. Catchers use a special heavily padded glove called a catcher's mitt. A first baseman uses an extra-large glove. It gives extra reach for bad throws.

Players' shoes are often called **spikes** (SPYKS). The metal or nylon points on the soles of baseball shoes are also called spikes.

Nylon spikes on the soles of baseball shoes are not nearly as sharp, or dangerous, as metal spikes. They are not, however, as useful on real grass as metal spikes. Nylon spikes are useful on artificial baseball fields.

Baseball gloves become like part of a player's hand. Spikes help a baseball player start, stop, keep balance.

UNIFORMS

Baseball players wear uniforms that include a brimmed cap; a shirt, or jersey; calf-high pants, or knickers; and high socks.

Each player wears a number on the back of the jersey and sometimes the player's last name. The team name or city appears on the front.

Many players wear one or two thin batting gloves. The gloves help a player grip the bat.

A catcher wears a face mask, chest protector, and shinguards in addition to the uniform.

Uniforms identify player and team. Major Leaguers' traveling uniforms show their city name on the front of the jersey.

MANAGERS AND COACHES

The person who runs the baseball team on the field may be called the manager or the coach. In professional baseball, the team leader is always a manager.

The manager or head coach decides who will play and in what position.

Third-base coach watches loose ball. With palm down he signals runner (green) to stop at third base.

Coach, catcher, and pitcher huddle to decide team's strategy for facing next hitter.

The manager also decides the batting order and the team's **strategy** (STRAT uh jee), or plan for winning. The manager, or head coach, uses hand signals to tell a hitter whether to swing, steal, or bunt, for example.

Coaches in the first-base and third-base coaching boxes help base runners plan their strategy.

UMPIRES

One or more umpires oversee a regulation game. Major league baseball games use four or more "umps." One umpire works behind the plate. Other umpires work first, second, and third base. In playoff games, umpires are added to the foul lines in left and right fields.

Umpires make decisions about fair and foul balls, whether base runners are safe, and balls and strikes. They rule on all plays, and they can stop a game or remove a player or coach from a game.

A Little League field has an outfield fence or wall about 200 feet (61 meters) around, keeping the same distance from the plate in left and right as in center.

An umpire keeps a baseball game moving under the official rules. The plate umpire here calls balls and strikes, among other things.

GLOSSARY

aluminum (uh LOO muh num) — a strong, hard, lightweight metal used in baseball bats

artificial (AHR tuh FISH ul) — looking or being similar to a "real" thing, such as artificial grass

dugout (DUG OUT) — a place for baseball players to sit below ground level at a baseball field

professional (pruh FESH uh nul) — related to a high level of skill, resulting in one being paid for that skill

regulation (reg yuh LAY shun) — that which is according to the rules: a baseball game played by the rules

spikes (SPYKS) — the sharp points on the sole of a baseball shoe, or the baseball shoes themselves

strategy (STRAT uh jee) — a plan or design

umpire (UM pyr) — any one of the officials on the field who make decisions about the game, such as fair or foul, ball or strike

Little League catchers wear helmets as part of the equipment that protects them from the baseball and bat.

110084

23

INDEX